Thomas Hardy

Pastoral Muse

First published in Great Britain by Brockhampton Press,
a member of the Hodder Headline Group,
20 Bloomsbury Street, London WC1B 3QA

ISBN 1 86019 392 7

Created and produced by Flame Tree Publishing,
part of The Foundry Creative Media Company Limited,
The Long House, Antrobus Road, Chiswick, London W4 5HY

Special thanks to
Kate Brown and Kelley Doak for their work on this series

Printed and bound in U.A.E.

Thomas Hardy
Pastoral Muse

Written and Compiled by
O. B. DUANE

Contents

Introduction

Hardy's poetry has always received less critical attention than his novels, but if asked to state his profession, without hesitation Hardy would have declared himself a poet, rather than a novelist. Although his first volume of verse was not published until he was fifty-eight, Hardy considered poetry his true vocation and frequently dismissed prose-writing as an economic necessity. When writing his novels, Hardy 'aimed at keeping his narratives close to natural life and as near to poetry in their subject as the conditions would allow'. He began to write poetry in the late 1850s, in his teenage years, and continued until his death at the age of eighty-seven.

Hardy grew up in the tiny hamlet of Bockhampton, three miles from Dorchester. His mother, who originally worked as a cook and housemaid, had been orphaned at an early age and had had a difficult upbringing. His father, a successful local mason, employed about a dozen men and was classed among the well-to-do village residents. The eldest of four children, Hardy was a frail child and was not sent to school until he was eight years old. His mother was very keen to encourage his interest in literature, however, and her young son could read fluently by the age of three.

Hardy was an outstanding pupil at school and particularly excelled at Latin. He completed his formal education at the age of sixteen and went to work as an apprentice architect in Dorchester under John Hicks; he was fortunate to find an employer who appreciated the old classics and permitted his workers leisure time for reading. Hardy continued to educate himself while he trained and it was during this period that he met Horace Moule, an extremely gifted Cambridge scholar, whose influence on him was profound. Moule, who later

served as the model for Jude Fawley in *Jude the Obscure*, became Hardy's close friend and mentor, encouraging him to read the Greek classics in their original form and introducing him to literary criticism and progressive theology.

By the time he moved to London for the first time in 1862, Hardy was determined to be a great poet and began writing earnestly in his spare time. He sent his verses to literary magazines throughout the capital but none was accepted for publication. For the next five years, Hardy worked under Arthur Bloomfield as an architect, but in time his lack of success as a poet, coupled with the tediousness of his employment, prompted him to return to Dorchester once more. He was still uncertain which career he should follow. He wanted to write, but his poetic endeavours had not brought any financial reward. Convinced that he would have little to lose by attempting to write a novel, Hardy began *The Poor Man and the Lady* during the summer of 1867 and, in doing so, set himself, quite unintentionally, on the path to becoming one of the most successful of all Victorian novelists.

Hardy's first novel was rejected, but his second, *Desperate Remedies*, was accepted for publication and sold reasonably well when it appeared in 1871. A third, *Under the Greenwood Tree*, was published a year later, meeting with 'a very kindly and gentle reception'. His first popularly successful novel, *Far from the Madding Crowd*, was published in 1874, and with the royalties he earned, he considered himself fit to marry Emma Gifford, a woman he had fallen in love with four years earlier while restoring the parish church of St Juliot in Cornwall.

Following the success of *Far From the Madding Crowd*, Hardy abandoned architecture and became a full-time novelist, producing an astounding number of highly successful and increasingly controversial works over a period of twenty-five years. His career as a novelist culminated in the publication of *Jude the Obscure* in 1896, a book which unleashed a vicious storm of protest, leading to its withdrawal from public libraries and widespread condemnation of its author as a thorough 'degenerate'.

With fourteen novels to his name, as well as several collections of short stories, Hardy was now secure enough financially to devote himself exclusively to his poetry, turning his back on an art form which had sustained him, yet brought him little or no artistic satisfaction. His first volume of verse entitled *Wessex Poems* appeared in 1898 and was largely compiled of poems he had written thirty years earlier, during his time of apprenticeship. To begin with, Hardy was not treated seriously as a poet and his work was scarcely tolerated by the critics. The *Saturday Review* printed an article in January 1899 criticizing *Wessex Poems* as 'slovenly, slipshod … stilted in sentiment, poorly conceived', but in the wake of his final novel's reception, Hardy had cultivated a healthy disrespect for the critics and remained unperturbed by their unfavourable reviews.

Having finally accepted that his progression from prose to verse signified a great deal more than an ageing writer's self-indulgent whim, critics were faced with the difficulty of trying to label Hardy's particular style of poetry. The attempt to compare him with other Victorian poets such as Swinburne or Tennyson, resulted in misunderstanding followed by dismissal, since Hardy's verse offered an unself-conscious view of reality compared to the Victorian's topical preference for a more decorative, abstract perspective. Hardy firmly believed that there was 'enough poetry' in what was left in life, 'after all the false romance had been abstracted, to make a sweet pattern'. He did not consider himself a philo-sophical poet, but continually emphasized the importance of 'unadjusted impressions', seeking to penetrate his own experiences with a view to producing poetry of intense and candid emotion which was proud of its often imperfect form and entirely devoid of pretension. *The Ruined Maid*, written in 1866, is one example of Hardy's individual approach to his subject. The poet's decision to elevate a servantgirl-turned-prostitute to the status of heroine is entirely at odds with Victorian moral standards, but this concern is set aside in favour of an honest, humorous treatment of character and theme.

Between 1898 and 1928, Hardy published eight volumes of poetry, each offering a wide variety of themes and moods, in keeping with the poet's belief that everything was a worthwhile subject for his work. He wrote of war, nature, friendship, bereavement and, above all, love and marriage. *Satires of Circumstance, Lyrics and Reveries*, published in 1914, includes a remarkable series of love poems 'Poems of 1912-13' exploring the very private relationship between husband and wife. These verses were inspired by the death of his wife Emma Gifford, and are a vivid recreation of courtship days and the growth of a marriage which does not attempt to gloss over its imperfections. The collection *Moments of Vision and Miscellaneous Verses* which followed in 1917 contained some of Hardy's finest war poems, prompted by the outbreak of the First World War which came as a great shock to the poet. 'Before Marching and After' commemorates the loss of his cousin, Frank George, while 'In Time of "The Breaking of Nations"', describing three different, yet interconnected, pastoral scenes, perfectly captures the futility of war and the greater importance of human life over territorial gain.

Throughout his poetic career, critics were quick to accuse Hardy of being unnecessarily pessimistic in his approach, often because they were unable to cope with his acute sensitivity and accurate observation of life which ran 'counter to the inert crystallized opinion' supported by the vast body of them. Hardy wrote poetry right up until the month before he died and intended to publish his final volume of verse *Winter Words in Various Moods and Metres* on his eighty-eighth birthday. He did not live to see this happen, but according to his second wife, Florence, he died in 1928 satisfied that 'he had done all that he meant to do', and happy in the knowledge that he had firmly adhered to his own principles. 'The ultimate aim of the poet,' he wrote in *The Life of Thomas Hardy*, 'should be to touch our hearts by showing his own, and not to exhibit his learning, or his fine taste, or his skill in mimicking the notes of his predecessors.'

Author's Note

Almost a thousand of Hardy's poems have survived, not counting his extraordinarily long epic poem *The Dynasts*. This volume aims to provide an introduction to the poetic works of this prolific man and concentrates on some of the better-known and cherished verses. The reader should note that a large number of Hardy's poems are undated and the year in which they were published is no indication of when they were originally written.

Chronology

1840   Hardy is born on 2 June at Higher Bockhampton, Dorset, the eldest son of Thomas Hardy and Jemima Hand.

1848   Attends the local school run by Mrs Julia Augusta Martin. His mother gives him Dryden's *Virgil* and Johnson's *Rasselas* to read.

1849-53   Enrolled at Isaac Last's school in Dorchester.

1856-62   Apprenticed to the architect John Hicks. Meets Horace Moule, and studies the Greek dramatists with him. Reads Darwin's *Origin of the Species* and writes his first poem, *Domicilium*.

1862-5   Moves to London and works as an architect under Arthur Bloomfield. Begins to send his poems to various journals for publication but most are rejected.

1867   Returns to Dorchester and becomes engaged to his cousin, Tryphena Sparks. Begins his first novel (now missing), *The Poor Man and the Lady*.

1870-74   Meets Emma Gifford, his future wife and completes his *Desperate Remedies* followed by the novels *Under the Greenwood Tree, A Pair of Blue Eyes* and *Far From the Madding Crowd*. Breaks off his engagement, marries Emma Gifford and moves to Surbiton, Surrey.

1876-8   *The Hand of Ethelberta* is published in 1876. Moves to Sturminster Newton. *The Return of the Native* is published in 1878 and Hardy sets up home in London.

1880-5   *The Trumpet-Major* is published in 1880. During a serious illness in 1881, Hardy writes *A Laodicean*, and a year later *Two on a Tower* is published. Returns to Dorchester to supervise the building of his house at Max Gate where he makes his permanent home.

1885-97 *The Mayor of Casterbridge*, *The Woodlanders*, *Tess of the D'Urbevilles*, *Jude the Obscure* and *The Well-Beloved*, together with several collections of stories, including *Wessex Tales*, *A Group of Noble Dames* and *Life's Little Ironies* published.

1898   Hardy's first collection of poems, *Wessex Poems*, published.

1901   *Poems of the Past and the Present*, is published. Begins writing *The Dynasts*.

1904-12 The first part of *The Dynasts* published in 1904, followed by two subsequent parts in 1906 and 1908. *Time's Laughing Stocks* published in 1909. November 1912 his wife dies unexpectedly.

1914   Hardy marries Florence Emily Dugdale. *Satires of Circumstance, Lyrics and Reveries* published, including 'Poems of 1912-13'.

1917-22 *Moments of Vision and Miscellaneous Verses* appears in 1917 and Hardy begins work on his autobiography: *The Early Life of Thomas Hardy* (1928) and *The Life of Thomas Hardy* (1930). *Late Lyrics and Earlier* published in May 1922.

1923-25 Hardy is visited by the Prince of Wales in July 1923 and publishes a play in verse entitled *The Famous Tragedy of the Queen of Cornwall*. November 1925 sees the publication of *Human Shows, Far Phantasies, Songs and Trifles*.

1928   Dies on 11 January at the age of eighty-seven. Final collection of poems *Winter Words in Various Moods and Metres* published posthumously.

Domicilium

IT FACES west, and round the back and sides
High beeches, bending, hang a veil of boughs,
And sweep against the roof. Wild honeysucks
Climb on the walls, and seem to sprout a wish
(If we may fancy wish of trees and plants)
To overtop the apple-trees hard by.

Red roses, lilacs, variegated box
Are there in plenty, and such hardy flowers
As flourish best untrained. Adjoining these
Are herbs and escluents; and farther still
A field; then cottages with trees, and last
The distant hills and sky.

Behind, the scene is wilder. Heath and furze
Are everything that seems to grow and thrive
Upon the uneven ground. A stunted thorn
Stands here and there, indeed; and from a pit
An oak uprises, springing from a seed
Dropped by some bird a hundred years ago.

In days bygone –
Long gone – my father's mother, who is now
Blest with the blest, would take me out to walk.
At such a time I once inquired of her
How looked the spot when first she settled here.
The answer I remember. 'Fifty years
Have passed since then, my child, and change has marked
The face of all things. Yonder garden-plots
And orchards were uncultivated slopes
O'ergrown with bramble bushes, furze and thorn:
That road a narrow path shut in by ferns,
Which, almost trees, obscured the passer-by.

'Our house stood quite alone, and those tall firs
And beeches were not planted. Snakes and efts
Swarmed in the summer days, and nightly bats
Would fly about our bedrooms. Heathcroppers
Lived on the hills, and were our only friends;
So wild it was when first we settled here.'

Neutral Tones

WE STOOD by a pond that winter day,
And the sun was white, as though chidden of God,
And a few leaves lay on the starving sod;
– They had fallen from an ash, and were gray.

Your eyes on me were as eyes that rove
Over tedious riddles of years ago;
And some words played between us to and fro
On which lost the more by our love.

The smile on your mouth was the deadest thing
Alive enough to have strength to die;
And a grin of bitterness swept thereby
Like an ominous bird a-wing ...

Since then, keen lessons that love deceives,
And wrings with wrong, have shaped to me
Your face, and the God-curst sun, and a tree,
And a pond edged with grayish leaves.

Friends Beyond

WILLIAM DEWY, Tranter Reuben, Farmer Ledlow
late at plough,
Robert's kin, and John's, and Ned's,
And the Squire, and Lady Susan, lie in
Melstock churchyard now!

'Gone,' I call them, gone for good, that group of
local hearts and heads;
Yet at mothy curfew-tide,
And at midnight when the noon-heat breathes it
back from walls and leads,

They've a way of whispering to me – fellow-wight
who yet abide –
In the muted, measured note
Of a ripple under archways, or a lone
cave's stillicide:

'We have triumphed: this achievement turns the
bane to antidote,
Unsuccesses to success,
Many thought-worn eves and morrows to a
morrow free of thought.

'No more need we corn and clothing, feel of
old terrestrial stress;
Chill detraction stirs no sigh;
Fear of death has even bygone us: death gave
us all that we possess.'

W.D. – 'Ye mid burn the old bass-viol that I
set such value by.'
Squire. – 'You may hold the manse in fee,
You may wed my spouse, may let my children's
memory of me die.'
Lady S. – 'You may have my rich brocades, my
laces; take each household key;
Ransack coffer, desk, bureau;
Quiz the few poor treasures hid there, con the
letters kept by me.'

Far. – 'Ye mid zell my favourite heifer, ye mid
let the charlock grow,
Foul the grinterns, give up thrift.'
Far.Wife. – 'If ye break my best blue china, children,
I shan't care or ho.'

All. – 'We've no wish to hear the tidings, how
the people's fortunes shift;
What your daily doings are;
Who are wedded, born, divided; if your lives
beat slow or swift.

'Curious not the least are we if our intents
you make or mar,
If you quire to our old tune,
If the City stage still passes, if the weirs
still roar afar.'

— Thus, with very gods' composure, freed those
crosses late and soon
Which, in life, the Trine allow
(Why, none witteth), and ignoring all that
haps beneath the moon,

William Dewy, Tranter Reuben, Farmer Ledlow
late at plough,
Robert's kin, and John's, and Ned's,
And the Squire, and Lady Susan, murmur
mildly to me now.

In a Wood
FROM 'THE WOODLANDERS'

PALE beech and pine so blue,
Set in one clay,
Bough to bough cannot you
Live out your day?
When the rains skim and skip,
Why mar sweet comradeship,
Blighting with poison-drip
Neighbourly spray?

Heart-halt and spirit-lame,
City-opprest,
Unto this wood I came
As to a nest;
Dreaming that sylvan peace
Offered the harrowed ease –
Nature a soft release
From men's unrest.

But, having entered in,
Great growths and small
Show them to men akin –
Combatants all!
Sycamore shoulders oak,
Bines the slim sapling yoke,
Ivy-spun halters choke
Elms stout and tall.

Touches from ash, O wych,
Sting you like scorn!
You, too, brave hollies, twitch
Sidelong from thorn.
Even the rank poplars bear
Lothly a rival's air,
Cankering in black despair
If overborne.

Since, then, no grace I find
Taught me of trees,
Turn I back to my kind,
Worthy as these.
There at least smiles abound,
There discourse trills around,
There, now and then, are found
Life-loyalties.

I Look into My Glass,

I LOOK into my glass,
And view my wasting skin,
And say, 'Would God it came to pass
My heart had shrunk as thin!'

For then, I, undistrest
By hearts grown cold to me,
Could lonely wait my endless rest
With equanimity.

But Time, to make me grieve,
Part steals, lets part abide;
And shakes this fragile frame at eve
With throbbing of noontide.

The Subalterns

I

'POOR wanderer,' said the leaden sky,
'I fain would lighten thee,
But there are laws in force on high
Which say it must not be.'

II

– 'I would not freeze thee, shorn one,' cried
The North, 'knew I but how
To warm my breath, to slack my stride;
But I am ruled as thou.'

III

– 'To-morrow I attack thee, wight,'
Said Sickness. 'Yet I swear
I bear thy little ark no spite,
But am bid enter there.'

IV

– 'Come hither, Son,' I heard Death say;
'I did not will a grave
Should end thy pilgrimage to-day,
But I, too, am a slave!'

V

We smiled upon each other then,
And life to me had less
Of that fell look it wore ere when
They owned their passiveness.

In Tenebris 1

'Percussus sum sicut foenum, et aruit cor meum.' Ps. CI

WINTERTIME nighs;
But my bereavement-pain
It cannot bring again:
Twice no one dies.

Flower-petals flee;
But, since it once hath been,
No more that severing scene
Can harrow me.

Birds faint in dread:
I shall not lose old strength
In the lone frost's black length:
Strength long since fled!

Leaves freeze to dun;
But, friends can not turn cold
This season as of old
For him with none.

Tempests may scath;
But love can not make smart
Again this year his heart
Who no heart hath.

Black is night's cope;
But death will not appal
One who, past doubtings all,
Waits in unhope.

In Tenebris 2

Considerabam ad dexteram, et videbam; et non erat qui cognosceret me
.... non st qui requirat animam meam.' Ps. CXLI

WHEN THE clouds' swoln bosoms echo back the
shouts of the man and strong
That things are all as they best may be, save a
few to be right ere long,
And my eyes have not the vision in them to
discern what to these is so clear,
The blot seems straightway in me alone; one
better he were not here.

The stout upstanders say, All's well with us:
ruers have nought to rue!
And what the potent say so oft, can it
fail to be somewhat true?
Breezily go they, breezily come; their dust
smokes around their career,
Till I think I am one born out of due time,
who has no calling here.

Their dawns bring lusty joys, it seems;
their evenings all that is sweet;
Our times are blessed times, they cry:
Life shapes it as is most meet,
And nothing is much the matter; there are
many smiles to a tear;
Then what is the matter is I, I say.
Why should such an one be
here? . . .

Let him in whose ears the low-voiced Best is
killed by the clash of the First,
Who holds that if way to the Better there be,
it exacts a full look at the Worst,
Who feels that delight is a delicate growth cramped
by crookedness, custom, and fear,
Get him up and be gone as one shaped awry;
he disturbs the order here.

A Broken Appointment

YOU DID not come,
And marching Time drew on, and wore me numb. –
Yet less for loss of your dear presence there
Than that I thus found lacking in your make
That high compassion which can overbear
Reluctance for pure lovingkindness' sake
Grieved I, when, as the hope-hour stroked its sum,
You did not come.

You love not me,
And love alone can lend you loyalty;
– I know and knew it. But, unto the store
Of human deeds divine in all but name,
Was it not worth a little hour or more
To add yet this: Once you, a woman, came
To soothe a time-torn man; even though it be
You love not me?

The Ruined Maid

'O, 'MELIA, my dear, this does everything crown!
Who could have supposed I should meet you in Town?
And whence such fair garments, such prosperi-ty?' –
'O didn't you know I'd been ruined?' said she.

– 'You left us in tatters, without shoes or socks,
Tired of digging potatoes, and spudding up docks;
And now you've gay bracelets and bright feathers three!' –
'Yes: that's how we dress when we're ruined,' said she.

– 'At home in the barton you said "thee" and "thou",
And "thik oon", and "theäs oon", and "t'other"; but now
Your talking quite fits 'ee for high compa-ny!' –
'Some polish is gained with one's ruin,' said she.

– 'Your hands were like paws then, your face blue and bleak
but now I'm bewitched by your delicate cheek,
And your little gloves fit as on any la-dy!' –
'We never do work when we're ruined,' said she.

– 'You used to call home-life a hag-ridden dream,
And you'd sigh, and you'd sock; but at present you seem
To know not of megrims or melancho-ly!' –
'True. One's Pretty lively when ruined,' said she.

– 'I wish I had feathers, a fine sweeping gown,
And a delicate face, and could strut about Town!' –
'My dear – a raw country girl, such as you be,
Cannot quite expect that. You ain't ruined,' said she.

He Abjures Love

AT LAST I put off love,
For twice ten years
The daysman of my thought,
And hope, and doing;
Being ashamed thereof,
And faint of fears
And desolations, wrought
In his pursuing,

Since first in youthtime those
Disquietings
That heart-enslavement brings
To hale and hoary,
Became my housefellows,
And, fool and blind,
I turned from kith and kind
To give him glory.

I was as children be
Who have no care;
I did not shrink or sigh,
I did not sicken;
But lo, Love beckoned me,
And I was bare,
And poor, and starved, and dry,
And fever-stricken.

Too many times ablaze
With fatuous fires,
Enkindled by his wiles
To new embraces,
Did I, by wilful ways
And baseless ires,
Return the anxious smiles
Of friendly faces.

No more will now rate I
The common rare,
The midnight drizzle dew,
The gray hour golden,
The wind a yearning cry,
The faulty fair,
Things dreamt, of comelier hue
Than things beholden !...

— I speak as one who plumbs
Life's dim profound,
One who at length can sound
Clear views and certain.
But — after love what comes?
A scene that lours,
A few sad vacant hours,
And then, the Curtain.

The House of Hospitalities

HERE WE broached the Christmas barrel,
Pushed up the charred log-ends;
Here we sang the Christmas carol,
And called in friends.

Time has tired me since we met here
When the folk now dead were young,
Since the viands were outset here
And quaint songs sung.

And the worm has bored the viol
That used to lead the tune,
Rust eaten out the dial
That struck night's noon.

Now no Christmas brings in neighbours,
And the New Year comes unlit;
Where we sang the mole now labours,
And spiders knit.

Yet at midnight if here walking,
When the moon sheets wall and tree,
I see forms of old time talking,
Who smile on me.

At Casterbridge Fair

I
THE BALLAD-SINGER

SING, Ballad-singer, raise a hearty tune;
Make me forget that there was ever a one
I walked with in the meek light of the moon
When the day's work was done.

Rhyme, Ballad-rhymer, start a country song;
Make me forget that she whom I loved well
Swore she would love me dearly, love me long,
Then – what I cannot tell!

Sing, Ballad-singer, from your little book;
Make me forget those heart-breaks, achings, fears;
Make me forget her name, her sweet sweet look –
Make me forget her tears.

II
FORMER BEAUTIES

THESE market-dames, mid-aged, with lips thin-drawn,
And tissues sere,
Are they the ones we loved in years agone,
And courted here?

Are these the muslined pink young things to whom
We vowed and swore
In nooks on summer Sundays by the Froom,
Or Budmouth shore?

Do they remember those gay tunes we trod
Clasped on the green;
Aye; trod till moonlight set on the beaten sod
A satin sheen?

They must forget, forget! They cannot know
What once they were,
Or memory would transfigure them, and show
Them always fair.

Her Definition

I LINGERED through the night to break of day,
 Nor once did sleep extend a wing to me,
  Intently busied with a vast array
 Of epithets that should outfigure thee.

Full-featured terms – all fitless – hastened by,
And this sole speech remained: 'That maiden mine!' –
 Debarred from due description then did I
 Perceive the indefinite phrase could yet define.

As common chests encasing wares of price
 Are borne with tenderness through halls of state,
  For what they cover, so the poor device
 Of homely wording I could tolerate,
  Knowing its unadornment held as freight
 The sweetest image outside Paradise.

Shut Out That Moon

CLOSE UP the casement, draw the blind,
Shut out that stealing moon,
She wears too much the guise she wore
Before our lutes were strewn
With years-deep dust, and names we read
On a white stone were hewn.

Step not forth on the dew-dashed lawn
To view the Lady's Chair,
Immense Orion's glittering form,
The Less and Greater Bear:
Stay in; to such sights we were drawn
When faded ones were fair.

Brush not the bough for midnight scents
That come forth lingeringly,
And wake the same sweet sentiments
They breathed to you and me
When living seemed a laugh, and love
All it was said to be.

Within the common lamp-lit room
Prison my eyes and thought;
Let dingy details crudely loom,
Mechanic speech be wrought:
Too fragrant was Life's early bloom,
Too tart the fruit it brought!

1967

IN FIVE-SCORE summers! All new eyes,
New minds, new modes, new fools, new wise;
New woes to weep, new joys to prize;

With nothing left of me and you
In that live century's vivid view
Beyond a pinch of dust or two;

A century which, if not sublime,
Will show, I doubt not, at its prime,
A scope above this blinkered time.

—Yet what to me how far above?
For I would only ask thereof
That thy worm should be my worm, Love!

The Year's Awakening

HOW DO you know that the Pilgrim track
Along the belting zodiac
Swept by the sun in his seeming rounds
Is traced by now to the Fishes' bounds
And into the Ram, when weeks of cloud
Have wrapt the sky in a clammy shroud,
And never as yet a tint of spring
Has shown in the Earth's apparelling;
O vespering bird, how do you know,
How do you know?

How do you know, deep underground,
Hid in your bed from sight and sound,
Without a turn in temperature,
With weather life can scarce endure,
That light has won a fraction's strength,
And day put on some moments' length,
Whereof in merest rote will come,
Weeks hence, mild airs that do not numb;
O crocus root, how do you know,
How do you know?

Channel Firing

THAT NIGHT your great guns, unawares,
Shook all our coffins as we lay,
And broke the chancel window-squares,
We thought it was the Judgement-day

And sat upright. While drearisome
Arose the howl of wakened hounds:
The mouse let fall the altar-crumb,
The worms drew back into the mounds,

The glebe cow drooled. Till God called, 'No;
It's gunnery practice out at sea
Just as before you went below;
The world is as it used to be:

'All nations striving strong to make
Red war yet redder. Mad as hatters
They do no more for Christés sake
Than you who are helpless in such matters.

'That this is not the judgement-hour
For some of them's a blessed thing,
For if it were they'd have to scour
Hell's floor for so much threatening ....

'Ha, ha. It will be warmer when
I blow the trumpet (if indeed
I ever do; for you are men,
And rest eternal sorely need).'

So down we lay again. 'I wonder,
Will the world ever saner be,'
Said one, 'than when He sent us under
In our indifferent century!'

And many a skeleton shook his head.
'Instead of preaching forty year,'
My neighbour Parson Thirdly said,
'I wish I had stuck to pipes and beer.'

Again the guns disturbed the hour,
Roaring their readiness to avenge,
As far inland as Stourton Tower,
And Camelot, and starlit Stonehenge.

The Torn Letter

I

I TORE your letter into strips
No bigger than the airy feathers
That ducks preen out in changing weathers
Upon the shifting ripple-tips.

II

In darkness on my bed alone
I seemed to see you in a vision,
And hear you say: 'Why this derision
Of one drawn to you, though unknown?'

III

Yes, eve's quick mood had run its course,
The night had cooled my hasty madness;
I suffered a regretful sadness
Which deepened into real remorse.

IV

I thought what pensive patient days
A soul must know of grain so tender,
How much of good must grace the sender
Of such sweet words in such bright phrase.

V

Uprising then, as things unpriced
I sought each fragment, patched and mended;
The midnight whitened ere I had ended
And gathered words I had sacrificed.

VI

But some, alas, of those I threw
Were past my search, destroyed for ever:
They were your name and place; and never
Did I regain those clues to you.

VII

I learnt I had missed, by rash unheed,
My track; that, so the Will decided,
In life, death, we should be divided,
And at the sense I ached indeed.

VIII

That ache for you, born long ago,
Throbs on: I never could outgrow it.
What a revenge, did you but know it!
But that, thank God, you do not know.

The Voice

WOMAN MUCH missed, how you call to me, call to me,
　　Saying that now you are not as you were
When you had changed from the one who was all to me,
　　But as at first, when our day was fair.

Can it be you that I hear? Let me view you, then,
　　Standing as when I drew near to the town
Where you would wait for me: yes, as I knew you then,
　　Even to the original air-blue gown!

Or is it only the breeze, in its listlessness
　　Travelling across the wet mead to me here,
You being ever dissolved to wan wistlessness,
　　Heard no more again far or near?

Thus I; faltering forward,
　　Leaves around me falling,
Wind oozing thin through the thorn from norward,
　　And the woman calling.

Rain on a Grave

CLOUDS SPOUT upon her
Their waters amain
In ruthless disdain, —
Her who but lately
Had shivered with pain
As at touch of dishonour
If there had lit on her
So coldly, so straightly
Such arrows of rain:

One who to shelter
Her delicate head
Would quicken and quicken
Each tentative tread
If drops chanced to pelt her
That summertime spills
In dust-paven rills
When thunder-clouds thicken
And birds close their bills.

Would that I lay there
And she were housed here!
Or better, together
Were folded away there
Exposed to one weather
We both, — who would stray there
When sunny the day there,
Or evening was clear
At the prime of the year.

Soon will be growing
Green blades from her mound,
And daisies be showing
Like stars on the ground,
Till she form part of them —
Ay — the sweet heart of them,
Loved beyond measure
With a child's pleasure
All her life's round.

The Going

WHY DID you give no hint that night
That quickly after the morrow's dawn,
And calmly, as if indifferent quite,
You would close your term here, up and be gone
Where I could not follow
With wing of swallow
To gain one glimpse of you ever anon!

Never to bid good-bye,
Or lip me the softest call,
Or utter a wish for a word, while I
Saw morning harden upon the wall,
Unmoved, unknowing
That your great going
Had place that moment, and altered all.

Why do you make me leave the house
And think for a breath it is you I see
At the end of the alley of bending boughs
Where so often at dusk you used to be;
Till in darkening dankness
The yawning blankness
Of the perspective sickens me!

You were she who abode
By those red-veined rocks far West,
You were the swan-necked one who rode
Along the beetling Beeny Crest,
And, reining nigh me,
Would muse and eye me,
While Life unrolled us its very best.

Why, then, latterly did we not speak,
Did we not think of those days long dead,
And ere your vanishing strive to seek
That time's renewal? We might have said,
        'In this bright spring weather
        We'll visit together
Those places that once we visited.'

Well, well! All's past amend,
Unchangeable. It must go.
I seem but a dead man held on end
To sink down soon. . . . O you could not know
        That such swift fleeing
        No soul forseeing –
Not even I – would undo me so!

Where the Picnic Was

WHERE WE made the fire
In the summer time
Of branch and briar
On the hill to the sea,
I slowly climb
Through winter mire,
And scan and trace
The forsaken place
Quite readily.

Now a cold wind blows,
And the grass is gray,
But the spot still shows
As a burnt circle — aye,
And stick-ends, charred,
Still strew the sward
Whereon I stand,
Last relic of the band
Who came that day!

Yes, I am here
Just as last year,
And the sea breathes brine
From its strange straight line
Up hither, the same
As when we four came.

— But two have wandered far
From this grassy rise
Into urban roar
Where no picnics are,
And one — has shut her eyes
For evermore

At Castle Boterel

AS I drive to the junction of lane and highway,
And the drizzle bedrenches the waggonette,
I look behind at the fading byway,
And see on its slope, now glistening wet,
Distinctly yet

Myself and a girlish form benighted
In dry March weather. We climb the road
Beside a chaise. We had just alighted
To ease the sturdy pony's load
When he sighed and slowed.

What we did as we climbed, and what we talked of
Matters not much, nor to what it led, —
Something that life will not be balked of
Without rude reason till hope is dead,
And feeling fled.

It filled but a minute. But was there ever
A time of such quality, since or before,
In that hill's story? To one mind never,
Though it has been climbed, foot-swift, foot-sore,
By thousands more.

Primaeval rocks form the road's steep border,
And much have they faced there, first and last,
Of the transitory in Earth's long order;
But what they record in colour and cast
Is — that we two passed.

And to me, thought Time's unflinching rigour,
In mindless rote, has ruled from sight
The substance now, one phantom figure
Remains on the slope, as when that night
Saw us alight.

I look and see it there, shrinking, shrinking,
I look back at it amid the rain
For the very last time; for my sand is sinking,
And I shall traverse old love's domain
Never again.

The Walk

YOU DID not walk with me
Of late to the hill-top tree
By the gated ways,
As in earlier days;
You were weak and lame,
So you never came,
And I went alone, and I did not mind,
Not thinking of you as left behind.

I walked up there to-day
Just in the former way;
Surveyed around
The familiar ground
By myself again:
What difference, then?
Only that underlying sense
Of the look of a room on returning thence.

The Two Soldiers

JUST AT the corner of the wall
We met – yes, he and I –
Who had not faced in camp or hall
Since we bade home good-bye,
And what once happened came back – all –
Out of those years gone by;

And that strange woman whom we knew
And loved – long dead and gone,
Whose poor half-perished residue,
Tombless and trod, lay yon,
But at this moment to our view
Rose like a phantom wan!

And in his fixed face I could see,
Lit by a lurid shine,
The drama re-enact which she
Had dyed incarnadine
For us, and more. And doubtless he
Beheld it too in mine.

A start, as at one slightly known;
And with an indifferent air
We passed, without a sign being shown
That, as it real were,
A memory-acted scene had thrown
Its tragic shadow there.

The Workbox

'SEE, HERE'S the workbox, little workbox, little wife,
　　That I made of polished oak.'
　He was a joiner, of village life;
　　She came of borough folk.

　He holds the present up to her
　　As with a smile she nears
　And answers to the profferer,
　　''Twill last all my sewing years!'

　'I warrant it will. And longer too.
　　'Tis a scantling that I got
　Off poor John Wayward's coffin, who
　　Died of they knew not what.

'The shingled pattern that seems to cease
　　Against your box's rim
　Continues right on in the piece
　　That's underground with him.

　'And while I worked it made me think
　　Of timber's varied doom;
　One inch where people eat and drink,
　　The next inch in a tomb.

　'But why do you look so white, my dear,
　　And turn aside your face?
　You knew not that good lad, I fear,
　Though he came from your native place?'

'How could I know that good young man,
That he came from my native town,
When he must have left far earlier than
I was a woman grown?'

'Ah, no. I should have understood!
It shocked you that I gave
To you one end of a piece of wood
Whose other is in a grave?'

'Don't, dear, despise my intellect,
Mere accidental things
Of·that sort never have effect
On my imaginings.'

Yet still her lips were limp and wan,
Her face still held aside,
As if she had known not only John,
But known of what he died.

The Wistful Lady

'LOVE, WHILE you were away there came to me –
From whence I cannot tell –
A plaintive lady pale and passionless,
Who laid her eyes upon me critically,
And weighed me with a wearing wistfulness,
As if she knew me well.'

'I saw no lady of that wistful sort
As I came riding home.
Perhaps she was some dame the Fates constrain
By memories sadder than she can support,
Or by unhappy vacancy of brain,
To leave her roof and roam?'

'Ah, but she knew me. And before this time
I have seen her, lending ear
To my light outdoor words, and pondering each,
Her frail white finger swayed in pantomime,
As if she fain would close with me in speech,
And yet would not come near.

'And once I saw her beckoning with her hand
As I came into sight
At an upper window. And I at last went out;
But when I reached where she had seemed to stand,
And wandered up and down and searched about,
I found she had vanished quite.'

Then thought I how my dead Love used to say,
With a small a smile, when she
Was waning wan, that she would hover round
And show herself after her passing day
To any newer Love I might have found,
But show her not to me.

The Blinded Bird

SO ZESTFULLY canst thou sing?
And all this indignity,
With God's consent, on thee!
Blinded ere yet a-wing
By the red-hot needle thou,
I stand and wonder how
So zestfully thou canst sing!

Resenting not such wrong,
Thy grievous pain forgot,
Eternal dark thy lot,
Groping thy whole life long,
After that stab of fire;
Enjailed in pitiless wire;
Resenting not such wrong!

Who hath charity? This bird.
Who suffereth long and is kind,
Is not provoked, thought blind
And alive ensepulchred?
Who hopeth, endureth all things?
Who thinketh no evil, but sings?
Who is divine? This bird.

An Anniversary

IT WAS at the very date to which we have come,
In the month of the matching name,
When, at a like minute, the sun had upswum,
Its couch-time at night being the same.
And the same path stretched here that people now follow,
And the same stile crossed their way,
And beyond the same green hillock and hollow
The same horizon lay;
And the same man pilgrims now hereby who
pilgrimed here that day.

Let so much be said of the date-day's sameness;
But the tree that neighbours the track,
And stoops like a pedlar afflicted with lameness,
Knew of no sogged wound or wind-crack.
And the joints of that wall were not enshrouded
With mosses of many tones,
And the garth up afar was not overcrowded
With a multitude of white stones,
And the man's eyes then were not so sunk that
you saw the socket-bones.

Kingston-Maurward Ewelease

Old Furniture

I KNOW not how it may be with others
Who sit amid relics of householdry
That date from the days of their mothers' mothers,
But well I know how it is with me
Continually.

I see the hands of the generations
That owned each shiny familiar thing
In play on its knobs and indentations,
And with its ancient fashioning
Still dallying:

Hands behind hands, growing paler and paler,
As in a mirror a candle-flame
Shows images of itself, each frailer
As it recedes, though the eye may frame
Its shape the same.

On the clock's dull dial a foggy finger,
Moving to set the minutes right
With tentative touches that lift and linger
In the wont of a moth on a summer night,
Creeps to my sight.

On this old viol, too, fingers are dancing –
As whilom – just over the strings by the nut,
The tip of a bow receding, advancing
In airy quivers, as if it would cut
The plaintive gut

And I see a face by that box for tinder,
Glowing forth in fits from the dark,
And fading again, as the linten cinder
Kindles to red at the flinty spark,
Or goes out stark.

Well, well. It is best to be up and doing,
The world has no use for one to-day
Who eyes things thus – no aim pursuing!
He should not continue in this stay,
But sink away.

The Oxen

CHRISTMAS EVE, and twelve of the clock.
'Now they are all on their knees,'
An elder said as we sat in a flock
By the embers in hearthside ease.

We pictured the meek mild creatures where
They dwelt in their strawy pen,
Nor did it occur to one of us there
To doubt they were kneeling then.

So fair a fancy few would weave
In these years! Yet, I feel,
If someone said on Christmas Eve,
'Come; see the oxen kneel

'In the lonely barton by yonder coomb
Our childhood used to know,'
I should go with him in the gloom,
Hoping it might be so.

Before Marching and After

ORION SWUNG southward aslant
Where the starved Egdon pine-trees had thinned,
The Pleiads aloft seemed to pant
With the heather that twitched in the wind;
But he looked on indifferent to sights such as these,
Unswayed by love, friendship, home joy or home sorrow,
And wondered to what he would march on the morrow.

The crazed household-clock with its whirr
Rang midnight within as he stood,
He heard the low sighing of her
Who had striven from his birth for his good;
But he still only asked the spring starlight, the breeze,
What great thing or small thing his history would borrow
From that Game with Death he would play on the morrow.

When the heath wore the robe of late summer,
And the fuchsia-bells, hot in the sun,
Hung red by the door, a quick comer
Brought tidings that marching was done
For him who had joined in that game overseas
Where Death stood to win, though his name was to borrow
A brightness therefrom not to fade on the morrow.

Afterwards

WHEN THE Present has latched its postern
behind my tremulous stay,
And the May month flaps its glad green
leaves like wings,
Delicate-filmed as new-spun silk, will
the neighbours say,
'He was a man who used to notice
such things'?

If it be in the dusk when, like an
eyelid's soundless blink,
The dewfall-hawk comes crossing
the shades to alight
Upon the wind-warped upland thorn,
a gazer may think,
'To him this must have been
a familiar sight.'

If I pass during some nocturnal blackness,
mothy and warm,
When the hedgehog travels furtively
over the lawn,
One may say, 'He strove that such innocent
creatures should come to no harm,
But he could do little for them;
and now he is gone.'

If, when hearing that I have been stilled at last,
they stand at the door,
Watching the full-starred heavens
that winter sees,

Will this thought rise on those who will
meet my face no more,
'He was one who had an eye
for such mysteries'?

And will any say when my bell of quittance
is heard in the gloom,
And a crossing breeze cuts a pause
in its outrollings,
Till they rise again, as they were
a new bell's boom,
'He hears it not now, but used to
notice such things'?

In Time of 'The Breaking of Nations'

I

ONLY a man harrowing clods
In a slow silent walk
With an old horse that stumbles and nods
Half asleep as they stalk.

II

Only thin smoke without flame
From the heaps of couch-grass;
Yet this will go onward the same
Through Dynasties pass.

III

Yonder a maid and her wight
Come whispering by:
War's annals will cloud into night
Ere their story die.

The Curtains Now Are Drawn

(Song)

I

The curtains now are drawn,
And the spindrift strikes the glass,
Blown up the jaggèd pass
By the surly salt sou'-west,
And the sneering glare is gone
Behind the yonder crest,
While she sings to me:
'O the dream that thou art my Love, be it thine,
And the dream that I am thy Love, be it mine,
And death may come, but loving is divine.'

II

I stand here in the rain,
With its smite upon her stone,
And the grasses that have grown
Over women, children, men,
And their texts that 'Life is vain;'
But I hear the notes as when
Once she sang to me:
'O the dream that thou art my Love, be it thine,
And the dream that I am thy Love, be it mine,
And death may come, but loving is divine.'

A Night in November

I MARKED when the weather changed,
And the panes began to quake,
And the winds rose up and ranged,
That night, lying half-awake.

Dead leaves blew into my room,
And alighted upon my bed,
And a tree declared to the gloom
Its sorrow that they were shed.

One leaf of them touched my hand,
And I thought that it was you
There stood as you used to stand,
And saying at last you knew!

The Fallow Deer at the Lonely House

ONE WITHOUT looks in to-night
Through the curtain-chink
From the sheet of glistening white;
One without looks in to-night
As we sit and think
By the fender-brink.

We do not discern those eyes
Watching in the snow;
Lit by lamps of rosy dyes
We do not discern those eyes
Wondering, aglow,
Fourfooted, tiptoe.

The Weary Walker

A PLAIN in front of me,
And there's the road
Upon it. Wide country,
And, too, the road!

Past the first ridge another,
And still the road
Creeps on. Perhaps no other
Ridge for the road?

Ah! Past that ridge a third,
Which still the road
Has to climb furtherward –
The thin white road!

Sky seems to end its track;
But no. The road
Trails down the hill at the back.
Ever the road!

Nobody Comes

TREE-LEAVES labour up and down,
And through them the fainting light
Succumbs to the crawl of night.
Outside in the road the telegraph wire
To the town from the darkening land
Intones to travellers like a spectral lyre
Swept by a spectral hand.

A car comes up, with lamps full-glare,
That flash upon a tree:
It has nothing to do with me,
And whangs along in a world of its own,
Leaving a blacker air;
And mute by the gate I stand again alone,
And nobody pulls up there.

A Second Attempt

THIRTY years after
I began again
An old-time passion:
And it seemed as fresh as when
The first day ventured on:
When mutely I would waft her
In Love's past fashion
Dreams much dwelt upon,
Dreams I wished she knew.

I went the course through,
From Love's fresh-found sensation –
Remembered still so well –
To worn words charged anew,
That left no more to tell:
Thence to hot hopes and fears,
And thence to consummation,
And thence to sober years,
Markless, and mellow-hued.

Firm the whole fabric stood,
Or seemed to stand, and sound
As it had stood before.
But nothing backward climbs,
And when I looked around
As at the former times,
There was Life – pale and hoar;
And slow it said to me,
'Twice-over cannot be!'

A Sheep Fair

THE DAY arrives of the autumn fair,
And torrents fall,
Though sheep in throngs are gathered there,
Ten thousand all,
Sodden, with hurdles round them reared:
And, lot by lot, the pens are cleared,
And the auctioneer wrings out his beard,
And wipes his book, bedrenched and smeared,
And rakes the rain from his face with the edge of his hand,
As torrents fall.

The wool of the ewes is like a sponge
With the daylong rain:
Jammed tight, to turn, or lie, or lunge,
They strive in vain.
Their horns are soft as finger-nails,
Their shepherds reek against the rails,
The tied dogs soak with tucked-in tails,
The buyers' hat-brims fill like pails,
Which spill small cascades when they shift their stand
In the daylong rain.

Postscript
Time has trailed lengthily since met
·   At Pummery Fair
Those panting thousands in their wet
And woolly wear:
And every flock long since has bled,
And all the dripping buyers have sped,
And the hoarse auctioneer is dead,
Who 'Going – going!' so often said,
As he consigned to doom each meek, mewed band
At Pummery Fair.

He Never Expected Much
[or] A Consideration
[A reflection] on My Eighty-Sixth Birthday

WELL, WORLD, you have kept faith with me,
Kept faith with me;
Upon the whole you have prov'd to be
Much as you said you were.
Since as a child I used to lie
Upon the leaze and watch the sky,
Never, I own, expected I
That life would all be fair.

'Twas then you said, and since have said,
Times since have said,
In that mysterious voice you shed
From clouds and hills around:
'Many have loved me desperately,
Many with smooth serenity,
While some have shown contempt of me
Till they dropped underground.

'I do not promise overmuch,
Child; overmuch;
Just neutral-tinted haps and such,'
You said to minds like mine.
Wise warning for your credit's sake!
Which I for one failed not to take,
And hence could stem such strain and ache
As each year might assign.

Christmas: 1924

'PEACE UPON earth!' was said. We sing it,
And pay a million priests to bring it.
After two thousand years of mass
We've got as far as poison-gas.

He Resolves To Say No More

O MY soul, keep the rest unknown!
It is too like a sound of moan
When the charnel-eyed
Pale Horse has nighed:
Yea, none shall gather what I hide!

Why load men's minds with more to bear
That bear already ails to spare?
From now alway
Till my last day
What I discern I will not say.

Let Time roll backward if it will;
(Magians who drive the midnight quill
With brain aglow
Can see it so,)
What I have learnt no man shall know.

And if my vision range beyond
The blinkered sight of souls in bond,
— By truth made free —
I'll let all be,
And show to no man what I see.

Index to First Lines

Notes on Illustrations